The Power of Three:

Wealth, Health, and Success in Harmony

Introduction

Welcome to "**The Power of Three**," a guide designed for young adults and starter families eager to cultivate a foundation for both personal and financial growth. Inspired by real-life success stories and expert insights, this book offers practical, holistic strategies for a balanced life.

In today's fast-paced world, achieving a balance between wealth, health, and success may seem like a daunting task. However, it is essential for individuals, especially those who are just beginning their journey into adulthood or starting a family, to understand that these three pillars are interconnected and can be harmonized to create a fulfilling life. Wealth is not merely about accumulating money, but about fostering financial literacy and security that empowers you to pursue your dreams without fear. Similarly, health extends beyond physical well-being and encompasses mental and emotional resilience, enabling you to sustain energy and enthusiasm for your life's endeavors. Success, finally, is a personal and multifaceted concept that reflects personal goals, achievements, and a sense of purpose. By focusing on these elements together, you can build a life that not only meets traditional markers of achievement but also enriches your day-to-day experiences, providing a sense of joy and accomplishment.

My Personal Journey

Reflecting on my early experiences with budgeting, I recall a time when financial chaos ruled my life. Through trial and error, I learned that budgeting isn't just about numbers—it's a tool to achieve your dreams and reduce stress. This realization became a turning point for my financial success.

To truly appreciate the synergy between wealth, health, and success, it is vital to understand how each aspect supports and enhances the others. Financial stability provides the means to access quality healthcare and resources that improve physical and mental well-being. In turn, good health serves as a foundation for productivity and performance, enabling individuals to pursue and attain their ambitions more effectively. As we navigate the complexities of modern life, it becomes apparent that success is not a singular destination but a journey characterized by moments of growth, learning, and adaptation. This journey is enriched when supported by sound financial principles and robust health practices. Moreover, cultivating a mindset that values lifelong learning, adaptability, and mindfulness can further enhance one's ability to thrive amid changes. By acknowledging and nurturing these interconnected elements, individuals and families can aspire to a harmonious existence marked by continuous development and lasting satisfaction.

Chapter 1: Understanding Budgeting

The Basics of Budgeting

Budgeting is more than a spreadsheet; it's a roadmap to financial freedom. Learn why budgeting is essential, debunk common misconceptions, and overcome the fears holding you back.

Welcome to "The Power of Three," your essential guide to achieving a harmonious balance between wealth, health, and success. In today's fast-paced world, young adults and starter families often find themselves juggling multiple responsibilities, from career aspirations and financial commitments to maintaining personal well-being. This guide is crafted to provide you with the tools and insights needed to master this delicate balance.

Imagine a life where your financial goals align seamlessly with your personal well-being, and success is not just a fleeting moment but a sustainable journey. This is the vision "The Power of Three" aims to help you achieve. Drawing upon real-life success stories and expert advice, this guide is filled with practical strategies to empower you to take control of your life.

For many, the path to achieving harmony in these areas may seem daunting. Whether you're struggling with budgeting, trying to find time for exercise, or seeking fulfillment in your career, this guide will serve as your roadmap. It will reveal actionable steps to integrate financial stability, health improvements, and personal achievements into your daily routine.

Start your journey with us, and discover how aligning these three powerful aspects can lead to a more balanced and fulfilling life. With "The Power of Three," you are not just setting goals; you are crafting a future where wealth, health, and success coexist in harmony. Let's take this transformative step together and unlock the potential to thrive in every aspect of your life. Embrace the challenge, and let this guide inspire you to soar beyond your current limits.

The Benefits

- **Gain Financial Control:** Master your money.
- **Debt Reduction:** Pay off debts faster.
- **Achieve Freedom:** Pave the way to financial freedom.

Gaining Financial Control

Taking charge of your finances is one of the most empowering steps you can take towards a secure future. Financial control is not merely about managing expenses, but rather about establishing a proactive relationship with your money. It involves understanding your financial habits, setting clear objectives, and making informed decisions to achieve long-term stability. When you master financial control, you gain the ability to make choices that align with your personal values and goals, paving the way for future opportunities and reducing the stress and anxiety often associated with financial uncertainties. This section will guide you through the foundational steps needed to transform your financial mindset, equipping you with the skills to create a sustainable and rewarding monetary path.

Strategies for Debt Reduction

Effectively reducing debt starts with a clear understanding of your financial situation and a dedicated commitment to change. Begin by cataloging all outstanding debts, including credit cards, student loans, and personal loans, and prioritize them based on interest rates and balances. Focus on paying off high-interest debts first while maintaining minimum payments on all others. Implementing debt reduction strategies like the debt snowball or avalanche methods can provide structured paths towards eliminating debt. Additionally, consider adjusting your expenses to free up more money for debt payments, and explore opportunities for increasing your income, such as side jobs or selling unused items. Consistent effort and small victories in reducing debt can lead to significant long-term financial relief and freedom.

Achieving Freedom

Achieving financial freedom is about more than just having enough money to cover your expenses; it's about having the flexibility to make choices that enhance your quality of life without financial constraints holding you back. It enables you to focus on your passions, spend more time with loved ones, and pursue opportunities that excite you. "The Power of Three" aims to guide you on this journey by breaking down the steps necessary to attain financial freedom. We'll explore effective budgeting techniques, smart investing strategies, and disciplined saving habits. Together, we'll navigate the complexities of personal finance, giving you the confidence and knowledge to build a resilient financial future. Our goal is to empower you with the tools needed to transform financial independence from a dream into a concrete reality, opening doors to a life where the freedom to choose and create is at your fingertips.

"**The Power of Three**" serves as your comprehensive companion in the pursuit of an enriched life where wealth, health, and success are harmoniously intertwined. As you embark on this journey, remember that the integration of financial stability, personal well-being, and career fulfillment is not just a distant aspiration—it is an achievable reality. By following the insights and practical strategies outlined in this guide, you will be equipped to cultivate a lifestyle that embodies balance and sustained happiness. Let this be the beginning of a transformative path, empowering you to thrive in all facets of your life and unlocking a future brimming with endless potential and freedom.

Chapter 2: Setting Financial Goals

Crafting SMART Goals

Guide your goals with **SMART** criteria (**Specific, Measurable, Achievable, Relevant, Time-bound**). Discover how to align financial aspirations with personal values.

Setting goals is a crucial component of achieving success in any area of life, and this is particularly true in the realm of personal finance. Goals provide direction and purpose, serving as a roadmap for where you want to go and how you plan to get there. They help to sharpen focus by breaking down larger ambitions into manageable steps, making the journey towards financial stability less overwhelming and more attainable.

By setting clear financial goals, you create a framework that encourages discipline, motivation, and accountability. This not only aids in monitoring progress but also ensures that every financial decision made is aligned with your overarching objectives. Furthermore, goals empower you to take proactive control of your finances, helping to curb impulsive spending and prioritize long-term wealth building. Ultimately, the process of setting and achieving financial goals enhances your financial literacy, boosts confidence, and lays the groundwork for a future where your financial well-being is secure and your dreams are within reach.

Examples of Goals

- **Short**-term, like a vacation fund.
- **Medium**-term, such as a new car.
- **Long**-term, like retirement savings.

Starting and Structuring SMART Goals

To effectively start and structure **SMART** goals, it begins with painting a vivid picture of what you wish to achieve in your financial journey. First, reflect on what is truly important to you, considering both your current situation and future aspirations. Once you have a clear vision, break it down using the **SMART** criteria:

1. **Specific**: Begin by making your goal as specific as possible. Instead of setting a vague goal like "save money," identify a precise target, such as "save $5,000 for an emergency fund."
2. **Measurable**: Ensure your goal can be measured, allowing you to track progress and stay motivated.

This involves establishing milestones, such as "save $1,000 by the end of each quarter."

3. **Achievable**: While ambition is crucial, your goals should also be realistic. Assess your financial capacity and resources, modifying the goal to reflect what's genuinely attainable, such as saving a particular amount each month that fits within your budget.

4. **Relevant**: Align your goal with your broader life aspirations to ensure it matters to you. If travel is a passion, for instance, booking a dream trip might be a pertinent goal that drives you to save.

5. **Time-bound**: Set a deadline to create urgency and focus. Having a clear timeline, such as "achieve this goal within 12 months," helps maintain momentum and prevent procrastination.

By meticulously applying the **SMART** framework, you can create a robust structure for your financial objectives. It not only clarifies what success looks like but also maps out the steps needed to turn your visions into reality. This structured approach fuels persistence and fosters accountability, driving you closer to your financial aspirations effectively.

Examples of SMART Goals

Simple SMART Goal: Building an Emergency Fund

- **Specific:** Save $3,000 for an emergency fund.
- **Measurable:** Save $250 per month.
- **Achievable:** Allocate $250 from monthly discretionary spending to a high-yield savings account.
- **Relevant:** Having a financial safety net aligns with personal security and peace of mind.
- **Time-bound:** Achieve the $3,000 target in 12 months.

This goal is straightforward and provides clear steps to establish a solid emergency reserve, ensuring you're prepared for any unexpected expenses.

Complex SMART Goal: Investing for Retirement

- **Specific**: Increase retirement savings to $100,000 in the next five years.
- **Measurable**: Contribute $800 monthly to a diversified retirement account with a projected annual return of 7%.
- **Achievable**: Adjust monthly budget to accommodate an increased contribution by reducing discretionary spending and reallocating annual bonuses.
- **Relevant**: Securing a comfortable retirement aligns with long-term personal and family financial security.

- **Time-bound**: Reach this financial milestone within five years, reassessing investments annually to optimize growth.

This complex goal involves strategic planning and regular adjustments to align with investment growth, reinforcing long-term financial stability and readiness for retirement.

Conclusion

Embarking on your financial journey with well-structured goals is instrumental in paving the way for long-term success and security. By utilizing the **SMART** criteria, you can transform abstract dreams into concrete plans that are both actionable and achievable. As you navigate the dynamic landscape of personal finance, remember that setting and adjusting financial goals is an ongoing process that evolves with your life circumstances and aspirations.

This approach not only empowers you to make informed decisions but also provides a foundation for continuous growth and financial wellness. Let the insights and strategies shared in this chapter serve as your guide, ensuring that each step you take brings you closer to realizing a future filled with stability and prosperity.

Chapter 3: Creating a Budget

Building a budget is a crucial financial practice, whether you are a beginner just starting on your financial journey or an experienced expert managing complex assets. For beginners, crafting a budget acts as an introduction to financial discipline, offering a clear picture of income versus expenses. It helps to identify unnecessary spending, prioritize essential needs, and establish foundational habits that support savings and debt management. Beginners who learn to budget effectively often gain confidence in handling their finances, setting the stage for future prosperity.

On the other hand, for experts, a budget serves as a sophisticated tool for optimizing resources, tracking complex financial movements, and ensuring alignment with long-term goals. It allows experienced individuals to make informed decisions, respond to market trends, and adapt their strategies accordingly. Regardless of your experience level, budgeting provides structure and clarity, helping navigate financial waters with precision and foresight.

Building a budget involves several key steps that help in organizing and managing your finances effectively. First, start by gathering all financial statements, such as pay stubs, credit card statements, and bank account records, to get a clear overview of your income and expenses. Next, calculate your total monthly income, including all sources such as salary, bonuses, and any side jobs. After determining your income, list all your expenses, dividing them into fixed expenses like rent or mortgage payments and variable expenses like groceries, entertainment, and dining out.

Once you have a comprehensive list of expenses, categorize them to identify spending patterns and areas for potential savings. This can involve breaking down expenses into further subcategories, like essential and non-essential costs. The next step is to set financial goals —both short-term and long-term—that align with your priorities and motivate you to stick to your budget. With a clear picture of income, expenses, and goals, it's crucial to allocate your income towards essential living costs, savings, and discretionary spending, ensuring that your expenditures do not exceed your income.

Lastly, regularly track your spending and adjust your budget as needed to reflect changes in income or lifestyle. Utilizing budgeting tools or apps can simplify this process, providing real-time insights and keeping you accountable. Remember, a successful budget is not static; it should be reviewed and revised regularly to adapt to your evolving financial situation. This process not only aids in managing day-to-day finances but also empowers you to work towards achieving your financial aspirations with confidence.

Building Your Budget

Begin your budget with these steps:

1. **Track Income**: Know what you earn.
2. **Categorize Expenses**: See where your money goes.
3. **Set Spending Limits**: Tame unnecessary outflows.

Tracking Income

Tracking your income is the foundational step in building an effective budget. Understanding your income streams provides clarity about what resources are available to you each month. Start by identifying all sources of income, which may include your primary salary, freelance or gig work, bonuses, rental income, dividends, and any side hustles. Ensure you account for both regular and irregular income to get an accurate representation. It's important to record your income consistently to monitor any significant changes over time. To do this, create a detailed spreadsheet or use budgeting software to log each source, specifying whether it's fixed or variable.

This practice not only highlights the total income but also differentiates between consistent earnings and occasional windfalls. Having a comprehensive understanding of your income schedule allows you to forecast cash flow, plan for upcoming expenses, and allocate funds more efficiently.

Moreover, being well-informed about your income enables you to make proactive decisions concerning saving and investing, enhancing overall financial stability and readiness for unforeseen expenses or opportunities. Regularly reviewing and updating this information ensures that your budget remains a realistic reflection of your financial situation.

Categorizing Expenses

Categorizing expenses is a pivotal step in managing your finances effectively, allowing you to gain insight into your spending habits and pinpoint areas where adjustments can be made. Begin by listing your expenditures and dividing them into two main categories: fixed expenses and variable expenses. Fixed expenses are those that remain consistent each month, such as rent or mortgage payments, insurance premiums, and utility bills. These are typically predictable, making it easier to plan for them in your budget. On the other hand, variable expenses can fluctuate depending on your lifestyle choices and needs, including groceries, dining out, entertainment, transportation, and clothing.

To further refine your budget, consider breaking down variable expenses into essential and non-essential categories. Essential expenses are necessary for day-to-day living, such as groceries, healthcare, and transportation costs. Non-essential expenses, like going to the movies or buying new gadgets, often represent discretionary spending and can be adjusted more easily to improve savings. This granular approach helps you prioritize spending, ensuring that essential needs are always met while highlighting potential areas for cost-cutting.

Additionally, tracking your expenses allows you to identify trends and patterns, such as seasonal spending spikes or areas where you consistently overspend. By analyzing this data, you can make informed decisions on where to allocate funds more effectively, align your spending with your financial goals, and avoid unnecessary debt. Utilizing budgeting tools or apps can simplify this process, offering a structured way to log and review expenses in real time. Regularly revisiting your expense categories ensures that your budget remains responsive to changes in your income or lifestyle, fostering a more sustainable financial outlook.

Setting Spending Limits

Setting spending limits is an essential strategy for maintaining financial discipline and ensuring that your expenses do not exceed your income. By establishing clear boundaries for each category of spending, you can control your financial outflow and direct funds towards savings and investment goals. Start by reviewing your categorized expenses and identify areas where you can cut back. Determine which non-essential expenses are the most flexible and set reasonable spending caps that still allow some enjoyment of life's luxuries without jeopardizing your financial health.

Consider setting specific limits for categories like dining out, entertainment, and shopping. For instance, decide how much you're willing to allocate towards eating out each month and stick to that limit by planning meals and social outings in advance. Similarly, assign budgetary constraints to your entertainment activities, opting for more cost-effective or free options when possible. A key component of successfully managing these limits is to closely monitor your expenses using tools such as budgeting apps that offer spending alerts, helping you stay within your designated ranges.

Beyond curtailing discretionary expenses, it's also practical to evaluate whether any fixed expenses can be reduced, such as negotiating service contracts or seeking more economical utility plans. Periodically review your spending limits and make adjustments where necessary, taking into account changes in your financial situation or priorities. This proactive approach not only aids in preventing debt accumulation but also ingrains a habit of mindful spending, ultimately leading to greater financial stability and the achievement of long-term financial objectives.

Budgeting Overall

Incorporating the categories of tracking income, categorizing expenses, and setting spending limits into your budgeting process provides a comprehensive framework that enhances financial clarity, control, and foresight. Understanding and accurately tracking income allows you to establish a clear picture of the resources available to you, forming the basis for all subsequent financial planning. This foundational knowledge enables you to make informed decisions about how to allocate your earnings effectively.

Categorizing expenses, on the other hand, introduces structure and specificity to your spending habits by distinguishing between fixed and variable costs. This distinction not only helps in identifying areas where you can reduce spending but also ensures that essential needs are prioritized over discretionary wants. By carefully managing these categories, you're better able to align your spending with your financial goals, avoid unnecessary debt, and potentially increase savings.

Setting spending limits reinforces financial discipline across all expenditure categories, ensuring that you remain within your means. By establishing clear boundaries, you mitigate the risk of overspending, supporting both short-term financial stability and long-term wealth accumulation. The interplay of these three categories forms a well-rounded budgeting strategy, fostering an environment where financial goals are systematically met, and financial health is sustainably maintained over time.

Choosing a Method

Explore different budgeting approaches:

- 50/30/20 Rule
- Zero-Based Budgeting
- Envelope System

50/30/20 Rule

The 50/30/20 Rule is a straightforward and popular budgeting method that simplifies financial management by dividing your after-tax income into three primary categories: needs, wants, and savings. According to this rule, 50% of your income should be allocated towards needs—essential expenses that are critical for daily living, including housing, utilities, groceries, transportation, and basic healthcare. These are non-negotiable expenses that must be covered to maintain a stable lifestyle.

The next 30% of your income is designated for wants, which includes discretionary spending on non-essential items such as dining out, entertainment, hobbies, travel, and any other activities or purchases that enhance your lifestyle but are not strictly necessary. This category allows for personal enjoyment and leisure while ensuring that these expenses do not overwhelm your budget.

Finally, the remaining 20% of your income should be earmarked for savings, debt repayment, and investments. This portion is crucial for building an emergency fund, contributing to retirement accounts, paying off existing debt, or investing in opportunities that generate future wealth. By adhering to the 50/30/20 Rule, you ensure a balanced approach to budgeting that addresses both immediate needs and long-term financial objectives.

Zero-Based Budgeting

Zero-Based Budgeting (ZBB) is a meticulous financial planning method that requires you to justify every expense from scratch each month. Unlike traditional budgeting approaches that often base new budgets on previous spending, ZBB starts at zero and mandates that every dollar of your income is allocated with clear intention. This method involves identifying all income sources and then assigning every dollar a specific role or duty, whether it goes towards fixed expenses, variable costs, savings, or debt repayment.

The primary advantage of the zero-based budgeting technique lies in its capacity to promote heightened awareness and accountability towards spending. By requiring detailed justification for each expense, this approach encourages individuals to critically assess their financial priorities and eliminate unnecessary expenditures. It offers a structured way to redirect funds towards areas that truly align with personal financial goals, such as savings or debt reduction.

To implement ZBB effectively, it is essential to meticulously track all income and expenses, adjusting allocations dynamically as necessary, based on changing needs or financial situations. This method can be consistently revisited monthly to ensure that spending habits align with evolving priorities. The disciplined nature of zero-based budgeting makes it an ideal tool for those seeking to maximize savings and financial efficiency, offering a pathway to more informed and intentional financial decision-making.

Envelope System

The Envelope System is a cash-based budgeting technique designed to simplify spending by creating physical boundaries for various budget categories. To implement this method, first determine the categories for your budget, such as groceries, entertainment, dining out, and more. Next, decide on a monthly spending limit for each category. Once you've set these limits, withdraw the total cash amount needed for all categories and distribute the funds into separate envelopes, each labeled with its corresponding category.

As you go through the month, pay for all expenses within these categories using only the cash from their respective envelope. Once an envelope is empty, you cannot spend any more in that category until the next budgeting period. This tangible representation of your spending helps reinforce discipline and prevents overspending. The Envelope System is particularly helpful for those who struggle with credit card use or tend to lose track of digital transactions, requiring a more concrete, tactile form of budget management. By visually and physically experiencing the allocation and depletion of cash, individuals often become more conscious of their spending habits, facilitating better financial decisions aligned with their budgetary goals.

Why These Systems Work

The budgeting systems discussed—50/30/20 Rule, Zero-Based Budgeting, and the Envelope System—work effectively because they provide structured frameworks that empower individuals to take control of their financial resources. Each method requires intentional allocation of funds, which in turn fosters disciplined spending habits. By categorizing expenses and prioritizing needs over wants, these systems ensure that essential obligations are met first. They also promote accountability and informed decision-making about how money is spent, encouraging individuals to save and invest for future financial stability. The visual or numerical clarity they provide can also motivate people to track their progress towards financial goals, providing a sense of achievement and direction.

Why They Fail with Inconsistency

However, these systems can fall short when there is inconsistency in their application. The success of any budgeting method hinges on regular tracking and adherence to set spending limits. Inconsistent monitoring of expenses, failure to update or adjust budgets in response to changing financial circumstances, and lack of commitment can all lead to overspending and financial disarray. Life's unpredictable nature can also present challenges; unexpected expenses might derail even the most carefully planned budgets if allowances aren't made for flexibility. Moreover, if individuals view these systems as merely restrictive, rather than as tools for financial empowerment, they may be less inclined to consistently apply them, leading to potential failure in achieving desired financial outcomes.

Which System is Right For You

Deciding on a budgeting system that suits your lifestyle and financial goals requires a willingness to experiment and evaluate. Start by selecting one of the budgeting techniques discussed, whether it's the 50/30/20 Rule, Zero-Based Budgeting, or the Envelope System. Implement this method for at least a couple of months to reliably assess its effectiveness. As you engage with each system, pay close attention to how well it aligns with your spending habits and financial objectives. It's important to reflect on whether the method feels intuitive and manageable within the context of your daily life. However, remember that consistency is crucial for any budgeting strategy to deliver results; sporadic application will not provide an accurate measure of its potential benefits. Dedicate time to adapt the system to suit any unique needs or unexpected financial changes, and persist long enough to assess its true impact on your financial health. Through patience and diligence, you can discover a budgeting approach that not only fits but also enhances your financial stability.

Effective budgeting is a foundational element for achieving financial stability and independence. The strategies discussed—50/30/20 Rule, Zero-Based Budgeting, and the Envelope System—demonstrate the diversity of methods available to tailor budgeting practices to individual needs and preferences. Each system provides a unique framework for managing finances, encouraging intentional spending and savings. It is essential to choose a method that resonates with your lifestyle and financial commitments, as this will enhance your ability to stick to the plan and realize its benefits. Consistency, adaptability, and a proactive approach to financial management are key to successfully implementing any budgeting system. By fostering a deeper awareness of income and expenditures, these methods empower you to take control of your financial future, paving the way for planned savings, investment growth, and overall economic well-being. Remember, gaining mastery over your finances is a continuous journey, one where informed and conscious decisions will lead to significant long-term rewards.

Chapter 4: Managing Expenses

Managing expenses effectively is a crucial aspect of ensuring financial health and stability. This chapter will delve into the various strategies and tools that can be employed to oversee and regulate personal expenditures. By understanding the significance of distinguishing between fixed and variable expenses and identifying non-essential costs, individuals can better allocate their financial resources. Implementing mindful spending habits, tracking expenses meticulously, and using expense management tools are some of the key practices that will be explored. Through these methods, readers will learn how to maintain control over their spending, avoid debt accumulation, and achieve their financial goals with greater certainty and less stress.

Cutting Discretionary Spending

Find ways to reduce non-essential expenses and avoid impulse buys. Get into the habit of regularly evaluating your spending patterns and identifying areas where you can cut back. For example, try substituting expensive restaurant meals with home-cooked options or reducing costly subscription services by only choosing those that add value to your life. Developing a more conscious approach to discretionary spending will help free up cash that could be better used towards savings or investments. It also builds discipline and cultivates financial awareness, leading to more intentional spending habits over time.

Keeping track of expenses is crucial for identifying areas where you might be overspending or neglecting essential payments. By monitoring expenditures regularly, individuals can avoid surprises at the end of the month and stay accountable to their budgeting goals. There are various ways to track expenses, from traditional methods like using a pen and paper or an Excel spreadsheet to more modern options such as budgeting apps or online expense tracking tools. Find what works best for you and make it a consistent part of your financial routine.

Creating a Realistic Budget

A realistic budget is a powerful tool for keeping expenses in check. Start by tracking all sources of income and expenditures, including fixed costs like rent/mortgage payments, utilities, and insurance premiums, as well as variable expenses such as groceries, entertainment, and transportation costs. Ensure that every dollar has been allocated to a specific expense category, and do not forget to leave some wiggle room for unexpected costs. A budget that accurately reflects your financial situation will help you stay accountable and make informed decisions when managing expenses.

Utilizing Expense Tracking Tools

In today's digital age, there are numerous tools available to track expenses automatically. From integrated banking apps that categorize expenditures to standalone budgeting applications, these tools provide valuable insights into spending habits and patterns. Some even offer features like bill reminders and alerts for overspending, making it easier to stay on top of expenses in real-time. Taking advantage of these technologies can significantly simplify the process of managing expenses, allowing more time to focus on other financial priorities.

Managing expenses effectively involves a combination of mindful spending habits, regular expense tracking, and utilizing various tools and resources. By distinguishing between essential and non-essential costs, creating a realistic budget, and staying disciplined with discretionary spending, individuals can take control of their finances and pave the way for financial stability and success.

Lowering Fixed Costs

Lowering fixed costs can have a profound impact on one's financial health by increasing available resources for savings, debt reduction, and investment opportunities. Fixed costs, such as rent, utilities, and insurance, are generally unavoidable but can be reduced through careful analysis and strategic planning. For example, negotiating with service providers for better rates, downsizing to a smaller living space, or switching to a more affordable insurance policy can lead to significant savings over time. By reducing these consistent monthly obligations, individuals can relieve financial pressure and create a buffer for unexpected expenses. This additional financial flexibility allows for a more robust allocation of resources toward achieving long-term financial goals and enhances overall financial resilience.

Expense Tracking Software

Leveraging technology to manage expenses can streamline the entire budgeting process, making it more efficient and less time-consuming. Several software applications are tailored specifically for tracking expenses, each offering unique features to aid in financial management. Applications like Mint, You Need a Budget (YNAB), and PocketGuard are popular choices. Mint provides a comprehensive view of your financial life, automatically categorizing transactions and offering customized budgeting tips. YNAB focuses on proactive budgeting by helping users assign every dollar a job and adjust priorities based on real-time financial circumstances. PocketGuard simplifies tracking by providing a clear overview of how much money is available for discretionary spending after accounting for bills and goals. These tools not only track expenses but also facilitate goal-setting, making financial management less daunting and more organized.

Basic Expense Tracking Template

Creating a personal expense tracking system can start with a simple template that organizes your financial data. Below is a basic template that you can copy and use as a foundation for monitoring your spending:

Monthly Expense Tracker

Category	Budgeted	Actual	Difference
Housing			
Utilities			
Groceries			
Transportation			
Health and Wellness			
Entertainment			
Dining Out			
Education			
Savings/Investments			
Miscellaneous			
Total			

Notes:
- _____
- _____
- _____
- _____

Use this template to consistently record your expenditures and compare budgeted amounts against actual spending. Regular assessment will highlight areas for improvement, helping maintain financial discipline and achieve budgeting goals.

Embracing a Minimalist Lifestyle

Effectively managing expenses is a critical aspect of achieving financial stability and security. By implementing a strategic approach that includes tracking expenses, creating a realistic and adaptable budget, and utilizing modern tools and software, individuals can gain a clearer understanding of their financial situation. The key is consistency and commitment to this process, which enables better decision-making and enhances financial resilience. As financial circumstances change, continuing to review and adjust strategies will ensure that goals remain attainable, leading to long-term success and peace of mind in personal finance management.

Adopting a minimalist lifestyle can be a powerful strategy for those looking to simplify their financial lives and focus on what truly matters. Minimalism emphasizes the value of experiences over possessions, encouraging individuals to reduce clutter and only keep items that serve a purpose or bring joy. This approach can lead to significant savings as it discourages excessive consumerism and prioritizes essential spending.

By valuing quality over quantity, minimalism often leads to better financial choices, such as investing in durable goods that stand the test of time rather than succumbing to fleeting trends. Additionally, a minimalist lifestyle often includes decluttering regularly, which can also provide an opportunity to sell unused items and generate extra income. Through intentional living and mindful consumption, minimalism can pave a path to financial independence and a more meaningful life, free from the burden of unnecessary material possessions.

Chapter 5: Saving and Investing

Begin Saving Now

Start with emergency savings and prep for retirement. The earlier one starts saving, the more significant the impact of compounded interest over time. Emergency savings should cover at least three to six months' worth of living expenses and remain in a liquid account, such as a high-yield savings account or money market fund. This fund serves as a buffer against unexpected expenses and provides peace of mind during challenging times.

Once emergency savings are established, aim to save at least 10-15% of income toward retirement. Take advantage of employer-sponsored plans like 401(k)s and Individual Retirement Accounts (IRAs), which offer tax incentives and potentially free money through employer matching contributions.

Diversify Investments

Diversification is essential for a robust investment portfolio. By allocating funds across a variety of asset classes, industries, and geographic regions, investors can reduce risk while enhancing potential returns. Consider diversifying your investments with stocks, bonds, real estate, and alternative assets like precious metals or cryptocurrencies. Regularly reviewing and adjusting your portfolio based on market conditions and personal financial objectives is crucial.

A diversified portfolio not only balances income-generating investments with growth-focused ones but also supports both short-term and long-term financial goals. Additionally, consistently reassessing your portfolio ensures it remains aligned with your evolving financial needs.

Intro to Investments

Learn the basics of stocks, bonds, and mutual funds. Stocks represent a share of ownership in a company, entitling shareholders to a portion of its profits. The return on stocks can be unpredictable and tied to market volatility, making it vital to diversify your stock portfolio.

Bonds are debt instruments issued by corporations or governments that pay investors fixed interest rates over time. They tend to offer more predictable returns than stocks but may not keep up with inflation. Mutual funds pool money from many investors to purchase various securities, including stocks, bonds, and others, providing exposure to a diversified mix of investments while minimizing risk.

As with any investment strategy, it's crucial to research potential investments thoroughly and consult financial professionals before making decisions. Consider your risk tolerance and financial goals

Stocks

Stocks, often referred to as equities, are financial instruments that signify partial ownership of a corporation. When individuals purchase stocks, they essentially buy a piece of the company, which grants them the opportunity to partake in its financial success through dividends and appreciation in stock value. As a result, stocks can be a potent tool for wealth accumulation, though they are subject to market fluctuations and inherent risks. Investing in a diversified portfolio of stocks can help mitigate some of these risks, enabling investors to spread potential losses across different sectors and industries. It's important to conduct comprehensive research and possibly consult with financial experts when selecting stocks to align with one's risk tolerance and long-term financial objectives.

Bonds

Bonds are fixed-income securities that play a crucial role in balancing an investment portfolio. They are essentially loans made by investors to corporations, municipalities, or governments, which promise to pay back the principal amount on a specified maturity date, along with periodic interest payments known as coupon payments. These interest payments provide a steady income stream and relatively predictable returns compared to stocks, making bonds an attractive option for risk-averse investors seeking stability. Bonds can act as a hedge against market volatility, preserving capital during economic downturns.

Different types of bonds, including treasury, corporate, and municipal bonds, offer varied risk levels and returns, allowing investors to tailor their portfolios to meet their financial goals and risk tolerance. It's important to assess the creditworthiness of the issuer and the bond's maturity term when investing in bonds, ensuring alignment with one's overall investment strategy.

Mutual Funds

Mutual funds are pooled investment vehicles managed by professional portfolio managers who allocate the fund's assets across a diverse range of securities, such as stocks, bonds, and other assets. This diversification minimizes risk and offers investors exposure to a broad array of financial instruments without the need to buy each security individually. Investors purchase shares of the mutual fund, sharing in the profits and losses proportionately. One of the primary advantages of mutual funds is their accessibility, allowing both small and large investors to participate in the financial markets with varying levels of experience.

Additionally, mutual funds offer convenience and liquidity, enabling investors to buy or sell their shares relatively easily. With various types of mutual funds available—such as index funds, which aim to replicate market indices, or actively managed funds, which seek to outperform the market—investors have the flexibility to choose funds that align with their financial goals and risk tolerance.

Alternative Investment Options

Exploring alternative investment options beyond traditional avenues like stocks and bonds can provide diversification and potentially enhance returns. Real estate investing, for instance, offers opportunities to earn rental income and appreciate property value over time. It can include residential, commercial, or industrial properties, each with unique benefits and risks. Cryptocurrencies have gained popularity as a high-risk, high-reward investment, characterized by significant market volatility and the potential for substantial gains. Another intriguing option is investing in commercial real estate, which can offer attractive yields and can serve as a hedge against inflation. Additionally, buying into or acquiring a business allows individuals to become directly involved in operations, potentially increasing their wealth by growing the business's value. Each of these options demands careful research and consideration of one's risk tolerance and financial objectives before investment to maximize potential returns while managing risks effectively.

Conclusion

Investments play a crucial role in building wealth and achieving financial goals. It is essential to understand the basics of stocks, bonds, and mutual funds and how they can complement each other in a well-diversified portfolio. Conducting thorough research and seeking professional advice can help investors make informed decisions that align with their risk tolerance and long-term objectives. Additionally, exploring alternative investment options beyond traditional avenues can offer diversification and potentially enhance returns.

Remember to reassess your portfolio regularly to ensure it remains aligned with your evolving financial needs as you work towards your financial goals. With careful planning and smart decision-making, investments can be a powerful tool for wealth accumulation and financial stability.

So, it is crucial to keep researching and stay informed about the ever-changing investment landscape to make the most of your investments. The key is to have a long-term perspective, remain disciplined, and not let emotions drive investment decisions. By following these principles and staying invested for the long haul, individuals can potentially reap significant benefits from their investments over time.

So don't be afraid to start investing and take advantage of all the opportunities that the financial markets have to offer! Just remember to do your due diligence, consult with experts when needed, and stay focused on your goals. With patience and perseverance, you can build a strong portfolio that supports your financial well-being now and in the future.

Chapter 6: Overcoming Budgeting Obstacles

Common Challenges

Budgeting is a crucial aspect of personal finance that involves creating a plan for managing income and expenses. While budgeting can be highly beneficial in helping individuals achieve their financial goals, it's not always easy to stick to. Many people face challenges when it comes to budgeting, resulting in the inability to follow through with their financial plans. Understanding these common obstacles and developing strategies to overcome them is essential to successfully managing one's finances.

One of the most significant challenges faced by individuals trying to stick to a budget is procrastination. It's all too easy to put off creating a budget or reviewing it regularly, especially when life gets busy. However, procrastination can cause significant setbacks in achieving financial goals. It's crucial to set aside time regularly to create and review a budget, ensuring that it remains aligned with one's financial objectives.

Another obstacle individuals may encounter is a lack of discipline and self-control. With easy access to credit and the temptation of instant gratification through impulsive spending, individuals may find themselves overspending and unable to stick to their budget. Developing discipline and self-control is vital in overcoming this obstacle and staying on track with financial plans.

Identifying Pitfalls: Procrastination and Developing Resilience

One of the most common pitfalls people face when trying to adhere to a budget is procrastination. This tendency to delay or avoid managing finances can lead to overspending, increased debt, and a lack of clarity about financial health. Overcoming procrastination requires setting clear financial goals, breaking tasks into manageable steps, and establishing deadlines to create a sense of urgency. Another key strategy is to automate financial processes, such as bill payments and savings contributions, reducing the burden of manual oversight.

Developing resilience, on the other hand, involves cultivating a mindset that can withstand financial setbacks and bounce back stronger. Building a robust emergency fund is a foundational step toward resilience, providing a safety net during unexpected financial challenges.

Additionally, maintaining a flexible budget that can adapt to changing circumstances without derailment is essential. Resilience also involves continuous learning and adapting, whether it's acquiring new financial skills or staying informed about economic trends.

By identifying pitfalls like procrastination and focusing on developing resilience, individuals can better navigate the challenges of budgeting and stay on the path to financial stability.

We Are Human!

Several common obstacles can impede budgeting success, leaving individuals struggling to align their expenditures with their financial goals. Beyond procrastination and lack of discipline, which we have already discussed, financial setbacks can also pose significant challenges.

Unexpected expenses such as medical emergencies, car repairs, or job losses can disrupt even the most meticulously planned budgets. These unforeseen circumstances can force individuals to dip into their savings or take on debt, derailing their financial progress. Additionally, lifestyle inflation, or the tendency to increase spending with rising income, can subtly undermine budgeting efforts, as individuals may adapt to a higher standard of living instead of allocating surplus funds towards savings or investments.

Recognizing these obstacles and implementing strategies, such as building an emergency fund, practicing restraint, and prioritizing financial goals, can help individuals overcome setbacks and stay committed to their budget.

Strategies for Success

Developing resilience and finding accountability can help overcome these challenges when it comes to budgeting. Resilience involves having a positive attitude towards setbacks, learning from failures, adapting to changes, and remaining focused on long-term goals. By developing resilience, individuals can overcome procrastination and stay committed to their financial plans.

Finding accountability can also be instrumental in staying on track with budgeting. This could involve having a budgeting partner or joining a support group focused on managing finances effectively. Being accountable to someone else can help individuals stay motivated and disciplined when it comes to sticking to their budgets.

Additionally, setting achievable goals and regularly reviewing and adjusting the budget can also aid in overcoming obstacles. Breaking down larger financial goals into smaller, achievable milestones can provide a sense of accomplishment and keep individuals motivated to stick to their budget. Regularly reviewing the budget and making necessary adjustments based on changing circumstances or spending patterns is crucial in ensuring its effectiveness.

Stay Motivated

Finally, staying motivated is essential in overcoming budgeting obstacles. It's important to remember why you started budgeting in the first place and the long-term benefits it can bring. Personal anecdotes and success stories from others who have successfully managed their finances through budgeting can also serve as inspiration and motivation to stay committed.

While budgeting may have its challenges, developing resilience, finding accountability, setting achievable goals, and staying motivated are key strategies for success. With determination and discipline, individuals can overcome these obstacles and achieve financial stability through effective budgeting. So don't let anything hold you back from reaching your financial goals – start budgeting today! Remember that small steps are taken consistently over time.

The Importance of Practical Tips and Strategies for Successful Budgeting

Implementing practical tips and strategies is crucial for successful budgeting because they provide clear, actionable steps to help individuals stay on track with their financial plans. These tools serve as a guide to making informed decisions, simplifying the budgeting process, and addressing specific obstacles. Tips such as setting measurable financial goals, tracking expenses meticulously, and employing technology like budgeting apps can significantly enhance one's ability to manage finances effectively.

By breaking down complex financial management into manageable tasks, these strategies can alleviate the overwhelming nature of budgeting, making it more approachable and sustainable. Furthermore, they allow individuals to tailor their budgeting approach to suit their unique financial situations, accommodating fluctuations in income and unexpected expenses. In essence, practical tips and strategies act as the backbone of successful budgeting, empowering individuals to maintain financial discipline and steadily work towards their economic aspirations.

Practical Tips and Strategies for Successful Budgeting

1. **Automate Savings and Payments:** To avoid accidental overspending and ensure that savings goals are met, set up automatic transfers to your savings account and schedule automatic bill payments. This reduces the temptation to spend money earmarked for savings or necessary expenses.

2. **Use Budgeting Tools and Apps:** Leverage technology to make budgeting easier and more efficient. Many apps and online tools can track spending, offer insights into spending habits, and send reminders for bills or saving goals. Popular options include Mint, YNAB (You Need A Budget), and PocketGuard.

3. **Implement the Envelope System:** This traditional cash management system involves allotting cash into specific envelopes for various spending categories, such as groceries or entertainment. Once the money in an envelope is spent, no more can be used for that category until the next budgeting period.

4. **Set Clear, Achievable Goals:** Break down large financial goals into smaller, manageable milestones. Celebrate reaching these milestones to maintain motivation. For example, rather than aiming to save $12,000 in a year, focus on saving $1,000 monthly.

5. **Track and Reflect Regularly:** Regularly review your budget and expenditures to ensure alignment with your financial objectives. Reflect on where you've succeeded and where adjustments may be necessary, using this as a guide to refine your budget planning.

6. **Reduce Discretionary Expenses:** Identify areas where spending can be minimized without impacting your quality of life. This might include dining out less, canceling unnecessary subscription services, or finding thriftier entertainment options.

7. **Create a Flexible Budget:** Allow room in your budget for unexpected expenses and fluctuations in income.

Set aside a small buffer fund to accommodate any unexpected costs without derailing financial progress.

8. **Seek Support:** Share your budgeting journey with friends or a community that has similar goals. This creates a support network that can offer encouragement and advice while also holding you accountable.

By implementing these practical tips and strategies, you can overcome common budgeting obstacles and stay motivated. Developing a budget that is easy to follow and customized to your needs empowers you to achieve financial success and security, building a strong foundation for the future.

We've explored the essential components of effective budgeting, highlighting the importance of resilience, accountability, and motivation in overcoming financial obstacles. By setting clear, achievable goals and leveraging practical strategies, individuals can streamline the budgeting process and address common challenges with confidence. Implementing tools such as automation, budgeting apps, and systems like the envelope method offers structure and ease, enabling consistent progress toward financial goals.

Remember that budgeting is a personalized journey that requires flexibility and regular reflection. By staying committed and adapting strategies to fit unique circumstances, you set yourself on a path to financial stability and peace of mind. Embrace these insights, and take decisive steps to transform your financial landscape today.

Chapter 7: Strategies for Work-Life Balance and Mental Well-Being

Achieving work-life balance and maintaining mental well-being are essential components of a fulfilling and healthy life. In today's fast-paced world, the lines between work and personal life are often blurred, leading to stress and burnout. Hence, developing strategies to manage these aspects is crucial for overall happiness and productivity. This chapter delves into practical approaches that empower individuals to create harmony between their career ambitions and personal life.

By exploring techniques for setting boundaries, prioritizing self-care, and incorporating mindfulness into daily routines, individuals can enhance their quality of life, improve mental health, and cultivate resilience against the pressures of modern work environments. Embrace the journey toward balance and well-being, as it can lead to sustained success and personal fulfillment.

Mastering Balance

Mastering balance is an art that requires intentional effort and thoughtful strategies. In our increasingly interconnected lives, where responsibilities often spill over from professional realms into our personal spaces, understanding the dynamics of balance is essential. Achieving equilibrium between work and personal life not only enhances productivity but also enriches personal relationships, mental clarity, and overall well-being.

Balance isn't about achieving perfection in every area of life simultaneously; rather, it's about making conscious choices that align with one's values and priorities. Recognizing the importance of balance allows individuals to mitigate stress, increase satisfaction, and foster a greater sense of control over their lives. By prioritizing balance, individuals lay the groundwork for sustainable success and happiness, promoting a healthier, more fulfilling lifestyle.

Striking a balance between professional and personal responsibilities requires deliberate effort and strategic planning. Here are some tactics to manage these aspects effectively:

1. **Set Clear Priorities:** Identify and prioritize the most crucial tasks in both your professional and personal life. Use a priority matrix or list to differentiate between urgent and important tasks, ensuring that essential responsibilities are addressed first.

2. **Establish Boundaries:** Clearly define your work and personal time, and communicate these boundaries to colleagues and family members. Ensure work stays

within designated hours, and allow for personal time that is truly free of professional obligations.

3. **Schedule and Time Management:** Use a planner or digital calendar to allocate dedicated time slots for work tasks, family activities, and personal interests. This assists in visualizing your daily commitments and prevents over-scheduling or time clashes.

4. **Delegate and Outsource:** Recognize tasks that can be delegated to others, whether at work or home. At the workplace, entrust team members with tasks they're suited for; at home, share household responsibilities with family members or consider outsourcing services like cleaning.

5. **Adopt Flexible Work Arrangements:** Consider flexible work options, such as remote work or adjusted hours, to better accommodate personal and professional obligations. Flexibility can help reduce stress and increase productivity.

6. **Invest in Self-Care:** Prioritize self-care by including regular exercise, adequate sleep, and relaxation techniques in your routine. Taking care of your physical and mental health ensures you're energized and focused for both work and home roles.

7. **Practice Mindfulness and Stress Reduction Techniques:** Incorporate mindfulness exercises, such as meditation or deep-breathing practices, to maintain focus and diminish stress. These methods promote clarity and calm, aiding in effective multitasking and responsibility management.

By implementing these strategies, individuals can create a harmonious balance that supports both professional achievements and personal fulfillment. This equilibrium not only boosts productivity and well-being but also cultivates a life marked by satisfaction and resilience in the face of various demands.

Self-Care Integration

Practicing mindfulness doesn't have to be complex or time-consuming. There are straightforward ways to incorporate mindfulness into your daily routine, fostering a sense of calm and presence throughout the day. Here are some simple techniques:

1. **Mindful Breathing:** Take a few moments during the day to focus on your breathing. Close your eyes, inhale deeply through your nose, hold for a few seconds, and exhale slowly through your mouth. Do this for a few minutes to ground yourself and bring attention to the present moment.

2. **Mindful Eating:** During meals, take the time to savor each bite. Pay attention to the taste, texture, and aroma of your food. By eating slowly and consciously, you can enhance your dining experience and practice gratitude.

3. **Walking Meditation:** As you walk, focus on the sensations of your feet touching the ground. Be aware

of your surroundings—the sounds, sights, and smells. This practice can turn a simple stroll into a powerful mindful exercise.

4. **Mindful Listening:** When engaging in conversation, pay close attention to what the other person is saying without planning your response. Listen with empathy and presence, which not only improves your relationships but also enhances your mindfulness practice.

5. **Mindful Pause:** Throughout the day, take short pauses to check in with yourself. Notice any tension in your body and consciously relax those areas. These brief moments can help reset your mind and maintain mindfulness amidst busy schedules.

Integrating these practices into your routine can lead to a noticeable improvement in your mental clarity and emotional well-being, allowing you to navigate daily challenges with greater ease and presence.

The Importance of Mental Clarity

Having a clear mind is integral to mastering mental clarity, which is essential for effectively managing life's complexities. A clear mind enables you to process information more efficiently, make well-informed decisions, and tackle problems with innovative solutions. Without mental clutter, you can focus on tasks with enhanced concentration and reduced distractions, leading to higher productivity and a more structured approach to responsibilities.

Clarity of mind also facilitates emotional regulation, allowing you to maintain composure and make thoughtful responses in challenging situations. The ability to filter out unnecessary mental noise empowers you to prioritize what's truly important, fostering a sense of control and direction in both personal and professional domains. Thus, nurturing mental clarity is crucial for achieving a balanced, purposeful life.

The Personal Value Beyond the Workplace

In many work environments, employees can often feel like just another number in a vast system. Organizations, driven by metrics and productivity goals, may inadvertently prioritize outputs over individual well-being. This perception can lead to feelings of anonymity and undervaluation, where personal contributions seem overshadowed by the company's broader objectives.

Consequently, it's crucial to remember the importance of self-care amid the demands placed by such systems. Taking care of yourself is essential not only for maintaining personal health but also for ensuring long-term satisfaction and fulfillment. By investing in your well-being, you safeguard against burnout and enhance your overall quality of life.

Finding balance and embracing activities that nourish your mind and body can empower you to navigate professional landscapes with resilience and a strong sense of personal identity. This self-investment also ultimately bolsters your capability to contribute meaningfully within and beyond your job roles.

Mental Clarity in Business Ownership

Owning a business can indeed provide a greater sense of personal value and fulfillment, as it allows you to directly witness the impact of your efforts and the growth of your enterprise. However, this increased investment in your business also necessitates a heightened level of mental clarity. As a business owner, the stakes are significantly higher, and having a clear mind is crucial for making quick, unbiased decisions essential to your success. Emotional involvement can sometimes cloud judgment, leading to reactive rather than strategic decisions.

A cluttered mind can amplify stress and hinder your ability to innovate or adapt to changing markets. Therefore, maintaining mental clarity enables you to approach challenges and opportunities with a balanced perspective, ensuring that your actions support long-term growth and sustainability. This clarity not only helps in steering the business forward with confidence but also enhances your capability to lead effectively, fostering a work environment that encourages creativity and collaboration.

Conclusion

Integrating self-care and mindfulness practices into daily routines is pivotal for nurturing mental clarity and maintaining personal well-being. Whether within the workplace or as a business owner, the clarity of mind serves as a cornerstone for better decision-making and effective problem-solving. Emphasizing personal value beyond professional achievements fosters resilience and fulfillment, empowering individuals to navigate both personal and professional challenges with a balanced approach.

By prioritizing mental clarity and self-care, one not only enhances personal productivity and satisfaction but also contributes more meaningfully to organizational goals and personal pursuits. As we conclude this chapter, remember that a clear mind and a well-cared-for self are essential elements for achieving a harmonious and purpose-driven life.

Chapter 8: Cultivating Healthy Relationships and Community

Building Strong Connections

Effective communication is the foundation of cultivating healthy relationships and fostering a supportive community. Improving your communication skills involves more than just expressing your thoughts clearly; it also requires active listening, empathy, and openness to others' perspectives. Active listening allows you to truly understand and appreciate what others are communicating, creating a reciprocal environment of trust and respect. Additionally, expressing empathy involves acknowledging others' feelings and experiences, fostering a sense of validation and connection.

Building a nourishing support network entails forming connections with individuals who uplift and encourage each other's growth. This can begin by engaging with like-minded groups or communities, where shared interests and goals naturally lead to supportive relationships. It's important to be proactive in nurturing these connections by regularly checking in with friends or colleagues, offering assistance, or simply sharing experiences. Through intentional communication and a commitment to supporting others, you contribute to an environment where everyone feels valued and connected, ultimately enhancing both personal well-being and community strength.

The Importance of Relationships in Personal Growth

Healthy relationships significantly impact our mental, emotional, and physical well-being. Engaging in positive interactions with others can reduce stress levels, enhance mood, and even strengthen the immune system. Emotionally, strong bonds provide comfort and a sense of security, helping individuals navigate life's challenges more effectively. Mentally, supportive relationships encourage personal growth by offering diverse perspectives and constructive feedback, aiding in self-discovery and learning.

A supportive community plays a vital role in achieving personal and professional goals. It fosters a sense of belonging and motivation, empowering individuals to pursue their aspirations confidently. Within a community, members can share resources, knowledge, and encouragement, which can be invaluable for overcoming obstacles and seizing opportunities. This collective support can lead to increased innovation and resilience, as individuals draw strength from their connections.

Balancing individual growth with nurturing relationships involves being mindful of personal needs while investing time and effort in maintaining strong bonds. It's about prioritizing meaningful interactions and being present for others without compromising one's own development. By finding this equilibrium, individuals can cultivate relationships that enrich their lives while continuing to pursue their personal and professional aspirations independently. This harmonious blend ensures that both personal well-being and community strength are sustained, fostering an environment where everyone thrives collectively.

Building Strong Interpersonal Skills

Developing strong interpersonal skills is crucial for fostering meaningful and lasting relationships across all areas of your life. One of the most important aspects is active listening, which involves giving full attention to the speaker, understanding their message, responding thoughtfully, and retaining the information shared. Practicing active listening can prevent misunderstandings and build trust, creating a stronger connection.

Empathy is another vital component of interpersonal skills, allowing you to understand and share the feelings of others. Demonstrating empathy involves recognizing and validating the emotions of those around you, showing support, and responding with compassion. These skills are essential for deepening relationships and ensuring that people feel heard and valued. Effective communication varies across different types of relationships, and tailoring your approach is important.

With family and friends, personalizing interactions by showing genuine interest and expressing gratitude can strengthen bonds. In romantic relationships, open and honest communication, along with maintaining respect and affection, often enhances intimacy and understanding. In professional settings with colleagues, clear, concise, and assertive communication helps in collaborating successfully while maintaining professional boundaries.

Conflict resolution is integral to maintaining harmony in any relationship. Approaching conflicts with a calm demeanor, focusing on the issue rather than personal attacks, and seeking mutually beneficial solutions can preserve and even strengthen relationships during disputes. Utilizing problem-solving techniques such as compromise or finding common ground promotes a constructive resolution process. By employing these strategies, individuals can navigate conflicts effectively, ensuring that relationships remain healthy and productive.

Identifying and Cultivating Healthy Relationships

Recognizing the traits of healthy versus toxic relationships is a vital skill for maintaining overall well-being. Healthy relationships are characterized by mutual respect, support, trust, and open communication. Individuals in these relationships can communicate their thoughts and feelings honestly while feeling valued and heard. Conversely, toxic relationships often involve manipulation, excessive criticism, lack of support, and poor communication, which can lead to emotional and even physical distress.

Setting boundaries and communicating needs effectively within relationships is essential to ensure mutual respect and understanding. Clear boundaries help define acceptable behavior and protect personal space, making it easier to maintain individual well-being. To communicate these boundaries and needs, it's important to be assertive yet empathetic, expressing your desires and limits without alienating others. Being open and honest about what you need in the relationship fosters an environment of transparency and trust, reducing misunderstandings and friction.

Nurturing relationships that align with personal values and goals involves investing time and effort into connections that support your personal and professional aspirations. This means surrounding yourself with individuals who respect and encourage your growth, share similar values, or understand your vision. These relationships can provide encouragement, inspiration, and accountability, helping you stay focused and motivated. By prioritizing meaningful and aligned relationships, you create a supportive network that not only nurtures your personal development but also enhances your overall life satisfaction.

Importance of Community

Finding community support is a powerful step towards personal growth and a stable life. Start by identifying your needs and interests to locate communities that align with your aspirations. Online platforms offer diverse groups, from professional networks to hobby-based communities, where you can connect with like-minded individuals.

Local events and workshops are also excellent opportunities to meet people who share similar goals or experiences. Volunteering within your community can provide a sense of purpose while connecting you with like-minded individuals who are passionate about making a positive impact.

Engaging with these communities allows you to share knowledge, gain new insights, and receive encouragement from others on similar journeys. By actively participating and contributing, you not only build a strong support system but also reinforce a network of resources that fosters growth and stability in your personal life.

The Power of a Supportive Community

Belonging to a strong community can have a profound impact on personal and professional life. Networking within a community offers opportunities to connect with individuals who can provide valuable insights, introduce potential job prospects, or offer mentorship. Shared resources within a community, such as knowledge, tools, or collective skills, enhance individual capabilities and often lead to collaborative successes. Furthermore, the emotional support from a community creates a sense of belonging and reassurance, where individuals feel understood and accepted during both triumphs and challenges.

Finding and connecting with communities that align with your interests and values is essential for meaningful engagement. Online forums and social media groups tailored to specific hobbies or professions are excellent starting points. These platforms offer convenience and accessibility, allowing participants to share experiences and advice with others worldwide. Additionally, local groups or clubs often provide a more personal connection, enabling face-to-face interaction which can lead to stronger bonds. Professional organizations in your field also present opportunities for growth, offering workshops, conferences, and networking events that align with your career interests.

The role of community in fostering accountability and growth is undeniable. Being part of a group encourages individuals to set goals and stay committed, as community members serve as both motivators and accountability partners. This collective encouragement and the sharing of diverse perspectives promote personal development and innovation. A supportive community environment challenges its members to step outside their comfort zones, driving them towards their full potential and ensuring that growth is both sustained and holistic.

Building and Strengthening Community Bonds

Active contribution to a community requires deliberate engagement and a willingness to support the collective. Volunteering your time and skills is one of the most direct ways to make a meaningful impact. This could range from participating in local community service projects to offering your expertise to help organize events or programs.

Sharing knowledge by hosting workshops or taking part in educational initiatives also strengthens community bonds and empowers others. Being a mentor provides guidance and support to individuals seeking growth, creating a ripple effect that benefits the entire community.

To build trust and foster collaboration within groups, transparency and consistent communication are paramount. Establishing open channels for dialogue encourages members to share their ideas and concerns, promoting a culture of inclusivity and cooperation. Actively listening, valuing each person's input, and recognizing their contributions helps to create an environment of mutual respect. Establishing common goals also aligns the group towards a unified purpose, which reinforces trust and collaboration.

Celebrating diversity and inclusivity is crucial in cultivating vibrant and dynamic communities. Embracing different perspectives and backgrounds enriches the group's collective knowledge and innovation. Creating spaces where all members feel welcomed and represented fosters an atmosphere of acceptance and understanding.

Prioritizing diverse representation in leadership roles and decision-making processes further enhances inclusivity, ensuring that a wide range of voices contribute to the community's growth and sustainability. In doing so, communities not only thrive on their shared strengths but also cultivate resilience and adaptability in a diverse world.

Overcoming Challenges in Relationships and Communities

Dealing with misunderstandings, conflicts, and emotional setbacks is a natural part of any relationship or community dynamic. When disagreements arise, it is crucial to address them openly and constructively. Practicing active listening and empathy can pave the way for understanding differing perspectives, creating an environment where conflicts are resolved quickly and amicably. If emotions run high, taking a step back to reflect before responding can prevent further escalation and promote a more thoughtful approach to problem-solving.

Recognizing when it's time to let go of unproductive relationships is another essential component of maintaining healthy interactions. Holding on to connections that no longer serve a positive role can drain emotional resources and hinder personal growth. Assessing the impact of each relationship on your well-being and progress is vital. If a relationship consistently brings negativity or fails to align with your values and goals, it might be time to re-evaluate its place in your life.

Strategies for rebuilding trust after breaches in relationships or community dynamics involve a committed effort from all parties involved. Open communication and transparency are vital in restoring confidence, along with acknowledging past mistakes and taking responsibility.

Actions speak louder than words, so consistent, trustworthy behavior over time can help mend fractures. Encouraging dialogue and facilitating honest conversations about expectations and boundaries contribute to a renewed foundation of trust and cooperation. Cultivating patience throughout this process ensures that healing occurs naturally and sustainably, allowing relationships and communities to strengthen from past challenges.

Technology and Relationships

The advent of social media has profoundly reshaped how we initiate and maintain relationships, playing a pivotal role in modern community building. These platforms provide unprecedented access to connect with friends, family, and wider networks, regardless of physical distance.

They facilitate the creation of online communities centered around shared interests, allowing individuals to engage in meaningful interactions and collaborations. However, this digital convenience comes with challenges, such as the risk of superficial connections or the spread of misinformation. It's essential to approach online interactions with discernment, ensuring that relationships built through social media are genuine and grounded in trust.

In long-distance relationships or virtual communities, leveraging technology is key to maintaining close bonds. Video calls, instant messaging, and collaborative online platforms allow people to share experiences and stay updated on each other's lives, making geographical barriers less significant. Embracing these tools can lead to creative ways of spending time together, such as virtual game nights or co-watching movies.

Despite the benefits, it is crucial to remain aware of potential pitfalls. The tendency to compare oneself with the often-curated lives presented on social media can lead to feelings of inadequacy or dissatisfaction. To counteract this, individuals should focus on authentic interactions and prioritize quality over quantity in their digital engagements. Building mindful habits and promoting digital literacy can further enhance these online relationships, ensuring they are enriching and supportive rather than detrimental.

Building Self-Confidence Through Relationships

Supportive relationships play a vital role in enhancing self-esteem and confidence. When surrounded by encouraging friends and family, individuals tend to feel more valued and recognized, which fosters a positive self-image. Emotional support in times of doubt or insecurity can provide the reassurance needed to face challenges, reinforcing a sense of capability and worth. Moreover, these relationships offer a safe space where individuals can express themselves authentically, further building confidence in interacting with others both personally and professionally.

Accountability partners or mentors are particularly instrumental in fostering personal and professional growth. By providing guidance and constructive feedback, they help individuals navigate their goals and challenges more effectively. Mentors can offer wisdom gained from their own experiences, illuminating potential paths and pitfalls in pursuing ambitions. Accountability partners, on the other hand, help maintain focus and motivation by encouraging individuals to remain committed to their objectives. The presence of such allies creates an environment of support and accountability that propels personal development.

Learning from others' experiences and perspectives is another significant benefit of supportive relationships. Exposure to diverse viewpoints and insights can broaden one's understanding and inspire new approaches to personal and professional situations. Listening to stories of resilience and achievement from peers or mentors can serve as motivation, instilling the belief that overcoming obstacles is possible. In this way, relationships not only enhance self-confidence but also enrich one's journey with valuable lessons that contribute to growth and fulfillment.

Practices for Strengthening Relationships

Scheduling regular check-ins or quality time with loved ones is a foundational practice for nurturing strong bonds. Whether it's a weekly dinner, a monthly video call, or a simple text message to catch up, these regular interactions help maintain connection and demonstrate commitment. Consistent engagement fosters understanding and closeness, allowing relationships to flourish despite busy schedules or physical distance.

Practicing gratitude and expressing appreciation can significantly enhance the strength of any relationship. Taking the time to acknowledge and thank loved ones for their contributions and kindness shows that their efforts are valued and recognized. Words of appreciation, whether verbal or written, can bolster the emotional connection and convey that each person's presence is meaningful and impactful.

Being intentional about balancing giving and receiving in relationships ensures a reciprocal dynamic, where both parties feel supported and valued. This balance involves actively listening to and meeting each other's needs while being open to receiving help and support when needed. By maintaining equilibrium in the give-and-take, relationships can grow healthier and more resilient, fostering mutual respect and cooperation.

Cultivating Relationships That Foster Success

Successful individuals often attribute a significant portion of their achievements to the strong networks and connections they have built over time. These relationships serve as a foundation for professional growth and provide invaluable support, guidance, and opportunities. Whether through mentorships, collaborations, or partnerships, cultivating meaningful connections allows for the exchange of knowledge and resources that can propel careers forward.

In professional settings, building relationships is an intentional and strategic process. Mentorships are particularly effective, providing a learning environment where less experienced individuals can gain insights from seasoned professionals. Mentors offer guidance, share their own professional experiences, and help mentees navigate the intricacies of career advancement. Similarly, collaborations allow for pooling talents and expertise to achieve joint goals, leading to innovative solutions and shared success. Partnerships, whether within or across organizations, expand business prospects and establish a network of allies that can support strategic growth.

The concept of "relationship capital" is central to understanding the impact of these connections. Relationship capital refers to the value created through nurturing and maintaining professional relationships that can be drawn upon for mutual benefit. It emphasizes long-term success by focusing on trust, reciprocity, and understanding. By investing in relationship capital, successful people ensure they have a robust network to lean on during both prosperous and challenging times, enabling sustained growth and achievement over the long haul.

Conclusion

Relationships are the bedrock upon which personal and professional success is built. By fostering supportive, confidence-boosting connections, individuals can unlock new dimensions of growth and self-awareness. Whether through emotional support from friends and family or guidance from mentors and accountability partners, the quality of our relationships significantly impacts our journey and achievements.

Strategic investments in relationship capital not only enhance career prospects but also ensure a steady foundation of trust and support. As explored in this chapter, practicing gratitude, maintaining balance, and intentionally cultivating networks are essential strategies for nurturing meaningful relationships. Ultimately, these connections enrich our lives, providing the scaffolding for resilience, inspiration, and success.

Chapter 9: Self-Discovery and Resilience

Personal Exploration

Discovering personal strengths and values is fundamental to leading an authentic life. To begin this journey of self-exploration, it is vital to engage in introspection and self-assessment. This process involves reflecting on past achievements and experiences to identify recurring themes or skills that bring a sense of accomplishment and joy. Common methods include journaling, seeking feedback from trusted friends or colleagues, and completing strength assessments or personality tests, all of which help illuminate core competencies and natural talents.

Equally important is understanding one's values, as they guide decision-making and prioritize what matters most in life. Identifying core values involves examining issues that evoke strong feelings—whether positive or negative—and recognizing the principles that drive those emotions. These may include integrity, creativity, compassion, or independence. By aligning actions and goals with personal values, individuals can ensure that they remain true to themselves and derive deeper satisfaction from their endeavors.

Leading an authentic life consequently becomes about harmonizing strengths and values, making choices that reflect one's true self, and pursuing paths that align with personal beliefs. Whether in careers, relationships, or hobbies, authenticity nurtures inner peace and fulfillment, allowing individuals to contribute most meaningfully to their communities and achieve their fullest potential. Through ongoing self-discovery and alignment with values and strengths, living truly authentically becomes not just a goal, but a sustaining practice for lifelong growth and happiness.

Beyond Finance: The Broader Impact of Self-Discovery

Self-discovery is an empowering journey that extends well beyond the confines of financial success, influencing numerous spheres of life. In the realm of personal relationships, understanding oneself fosters better communication and stronger connections with others.

This self-awareness allows individuals to express their needs and boundaries clearly, leading to healthier and more fulfilling relationships. Moreover, knowing one's emotional triggers and responses can improve conflict resolution skills, reducing misunderstandings and fostering a deeper sense of empathy and collaboration.

In the professional domain, self-discovery aids in career development by identifying passions and areas where an individual can apply their strengths most effectively. It encourages proactive career choices and personal branding that align with one's authenticity, ultimately facilitating more satisfying and purpose-driven work experiences. Additionally, self-awareness can inspire leadership capabilities, as those who understand themselves are often better equipped to understand and motivate others.

Beyond relationships and careers, self-discovery enriches personal well-being by promoting mental health and resilience. Awareness of personal values and needs contributes to stress management and cultivates a more balanced lifestyle.

Engaging in practices like mindfulness or meditation, rooted in self-awareness, builds emotional resilience and enhances overall quality of life. Thus, the benefits of self-discovery permeate all aspects of existence, creating a holistic foundation for a life of balance, fulfillment, and sustained growth.

Building Resilience in the Finance World

Building resilience in the finance world involves navigating an ever-evolving landscape with adaptability, foresight, and strategic planning. Financial markets are subject to volatility, driven by economic cycles, geopolitical events, and technological advancements, which require professionals in the industry to maintain a steady composure and proactive mindset.

At its core, resilience in finance entails developing the capacity to withstand and recover from adversity, such as market downturns or unexpected disruptions. This process begins with cultivating a strong foundation of financial literacy and analytical skills, enabling individuals to assess risks effectively and make informed decisions.

Moreover, resilience in finance is fostered through continuous learning and improvement, as the sector demands the ability to quickly adapt to new regulations, tools, and methodologies. Networking and relationship-building within the finance community also play crucial roles, as peer support and mentorship can provide valuable insights and encouragement during challenging times.

Effective stress management techniques are essential, too, helping finance professionals maintain clarity and focus. By marrying technical expertise with emotional intelligence and strategic foresight, resilience in the finance world not only leads to individual success but also contributes to the broader stability and growth of financial systems.

Tools and Techniques to Overcome Obstacles and Recover from Setbacks

Developing resilience is crucial in navigating life's challenges and bouncing back from setbacks. Several tools and techniques can aid individuals in building this resilience. One powerful tool is maintaining a growth mindset, which involves viewing challenges as opportunities to learn and grow rather than insurmountable barriers. This mindset encourages perseverance and proactive problem-solving, fostering adaptability when faced with adversity.

Mindfulness and stress reduction practices, such as meditation and deep breathing exercises, are also effective in enhancing resilience. These techniques help in managing emotional responses, reducing anxiety, and improving focus, allowing individuals to respond to stress in a composed and constructive manner. Journaling is another valuable technique, enabling individuals to process their thoughts and emotions, gain perspective, and identify potential solutions to overcome obstacles.

Goal setting is a strategic approach to resilience, as it provides direction and motivation during challenging times. By setting realistic, incremental goals, individuals can maintain a sense of progress and achievement, even when larger objectives seem distant. Furthermore, seeking support from a network of family, friends, or professional counselors is essential. Having a reliable support system offers encouragement, new perspectives, and guidance, making it easier to withstand setbacks and pursue a path forward.

Ultimately, resilience is about building internal resources and external support systems that empower individuals to face challenges with confidence and emerge stronger from every setback.

Your Journey Ahead

Key Takeaways and Final Thoughts

As we conclude this exploration into the multifaceted journey of personal and professional growth, several key takeaways emerge. Firstly, self-discovery is a transformative process that enhances personal relationships, professional development, and overall well-being, serving as a catalyst for a balanced, fulfilling life.

Within the financial sphere, building resilience is essential for navigating an unpredictable landscape, utilizing tools such as continuous learning, stress management, and strategic networking. Furthermore, adopting resilience techniques ensures we can overcome life's obstacles and emerge stronger.

Now, we extend an invitation for actionable change: embrace budgeting not merely as a discipline but as the foundational step towards the life you envision. Begin by setting clear, achievable goals that align with your values and aspirations. Engage in continuous self-reflection and improvement, ensuring that each decision is a step forward in your journey towards happiness and success. Remember, the pursuit of financial literacy, mindful living, and emotional resilience is not just about coping with challenges—it's about thriving amidst them, crafting a future enriched with purpose and balance.

"The Power of Three: Wealth, Health, and Success in Harmony" underscores the profound interconnectedness of these three essential life pillars. Throughout this guide, we've explored how financial literacy, physical and mental well-being, and personal achievements are not isolated pursuits but components of a holistic approach to living a balanced and fulfilling life. By applying the strategies discussed, you can weave these elements into your daily routine, creating a synergy that enhances your overall well-being.

Remember, wealth is more than just financial gain; it is the security and freedom to pursue what truly matters to you. Health is not limited to the absence of illness but encompasses a state of complete physical, mental, and emotional resilience. Success, meanwhile, is a personal journey of growth and purpose, defined by the goals that resonate with your core values.

As you move forward, embrace the journey towards harmony with open arms. Allow the insights and practical steps from this book to guide you in crafting a life where wealth, health, and success are in seamless balance. Take inspired action today, and let this be the beginning of a transformative path that leads to a future filled with potential, happiness, and enduring satisfaction. With "The Power of Three," you have the tools to thrive and create a life rich in meaning and accomplishment.

Embrace your wealth, health and success in Harmony!

www.ingramcontent.com/pod-product-compliance
Lightning Source LLC
Chambersburg PA
CBHW071106240526
45469CB00006BD/2359